Caring for Y...

by Michèle D...

Pioneer Valley Educational Press, Inc.

Contents

Choosing a Dog

There are many kinds of dogs. There are
large dogs, medium-sized dogs,
and small dogs. What kind of dog
is best for you? Do you want a dog
with long hair, or short hair?
Do you want a puppy, or an older dog?
Your dog can be a special friend to you.

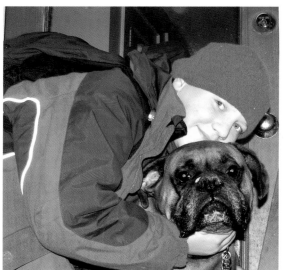

A New Home

When you bring your dog home, he might
be sad. An older dog might be missing his
old family. A puppy might cry
because he is missing his mother
and his brothers and sisters.
You can help your new friend feel better
if you sit down next to him
and say his name. Talk to him softly,
and this will remind him of his mother
and his brothers and sisters.

At bedtime, your dog might be unhappy. He might whine and cry. If he is a puppy, you can put a wind-up clock in his bed. The ticking of the clock will sound like the beating of his mother's heart.

When your new dog gets to know you, he will be happy to see you. He will jump up on everyone and chew on everything.

He will want to play.

He will like balls and toys that make squeaky noises.

This puppy jumps up. He wants to play! ▶

Caring for Your Dog

Puppies need special food.
Your veterinarian can help you choose food
that will help your puppy grow.
Feed your puppy small meals three or four
times each day. Since his stomach is small,
he should not eat too much at once, or he
will get sick.

When your dog is older, he will need only
one or two meals a day.

Your dog will also need fresh water. Fill your dog's water dish with clean, fresh water every day. A dog should have water to drink whenever he wants it.

Dogs love to chew on things. They will chew up anything they find. They love socks and shoes! Give your dog something good for him to chew on. You can give him a rawhide bone.

You can also buy your dog a soup bone at the grocery store. This kind of bone is safe for him to chew on. Some bones are not good for dogs. Never let your dog eat chicken bones or pork chop bones. These bones can break into splinters and hurt your dog. If your dog swallows a piece of bone, it might get stuck in his throat or stomach.

◀ *All dogs, young and old, love to chew.*

The veterinarian might want
to give your dog a check-up.
The veterinarian will check
to see if your dog is healthy.

When a puppy is two months old,
he will need to go to the veterinarian
for some shots. Older dogs will also need
shots to keep them healthy.

A veterinarian listens to a puppy's heartbeat. ▶

House-training a Dog

The best way to house-train a puppy is to use a special pen called a crate. At night, when you can't watch your puppy, put him in the crate. When you let him out to play, take him outside right away so he will not make a mess in the house. Your puppy will like his crate. Put a toy in the crate with a soft towel or blanket. Your puppy will want to keep his little room clean.

This puppy feels safe in his crate. ▶

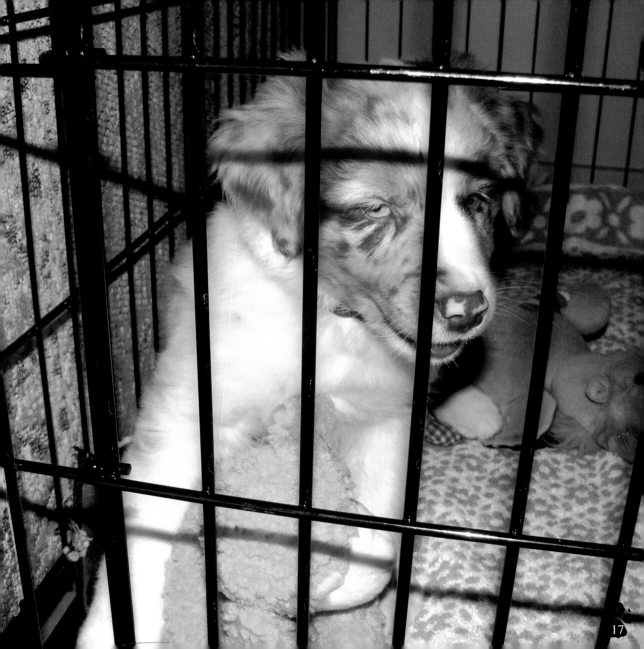

Pick a place outside for your dog to use as a bathroom. Take him to the same place each time. When your new dog goes to the bathroom outside, say "Good dog!" Sometimes a dog will make mistakes. When this happens, clean up the mess quickly. If a dog can still smell the mess he made before, he might make another mistake in the same spot.

A mistake should be cleaned up quickly. ▶

Training Your Dog

Start to teach your dog as soon as you bring him home. Keep the lessons short. Sometimes you can find a puppy kindergarten class where your puppy will learn some manners. By the time a puppy is six months old, he can learn to sit and stay. Some puppies will learn new things quickly, and others will need lots of practice.

This six-month-old puppy has learned to sit and stay. ▶

Always show your dog that you are pleased with him when he does what you ask. Do not shout or hit your dog. Just say "No!" when you are not happy. Your puppy will know if you are pleased or angry by the tone of your voice.

You can teach your dog to sit. Each time your dog sits down, say "Sit." Say the word slowly and clearly. After you teach him to sit, you can teach him to stay in one spot when you walk away. Put your hand out in front toward your dog's face. Say "Stay" slowly. Then slowly take a few steps back. Say "Stay" again. If your dog follows you, start over. Tell your dog to sit. Say "Good dog!" Then put your hand out and say "Stay!"

This dog has learned to stay. ▶

Next, teach your dog to come
when you call him. You can use
a long leash. Bend down so your dog can
see your eyes. Wait for a moment.
Then call your dog.
Say his name and then say "Come!"
Pull gently on the leash.
Your dog should sit at your feet
when he comes. Praise your dog
right away. Give him a hug
and maybe a small treat.

This dog gets a small treat as a reward for sitting. ▶

A Best Friend

Your dog will be happy when you come home from school. He will always want to run and play with you. He will know when you are sad and when you are happy. Your dog will become part of your family. Your dog can be your best friend.

This dog is very happy that his best friend is home from school. ▶

Glossary

crate: a cage-like container

puppy kindergarten: a class for puppies

veterinarian: an animal doctor